**lyit** | Institiúid Teicneolaíochta Leitir Ceanainn
Letterkenny Institute of Technology

Fontana
An Imprint of HarperCollins*Publishers*
77–85 Fulham Palace Road
Hammersmith, London W6 8JB

Published by Fontana 1991
9 8 7 6 5 4 3 2

First published in Great Britain by
Angus & Robertson (UK) 1988
Reprinted five times

Copyright © Kathleen Keating 1988
Drawings by Mimi Noland © Compcare Productions

The Author assets the moral right to
be identified as the author of this work

ISBN 0 00 637801 3

Printed in Great Britain by
HarperCollinsManufacturing Glasgow

# THE
# SECOND
# LITTLE BOOK OF
# HUGS

Kathleen Keating

Drawings by Mimi Noland

Fontana
*An Imprint of* HarperCollins*Publishers*

I embrace with honor
my father and mother, Roy and Minnie Armistead
my sister, Christine Ann Armistead

I embrace with gratitude
Helen Colton, for inspiring me

My friends Lynne and Maureen De Boer, Margie
Rinehart, Wendy McCarty Wong, Anita Liggett,
Francie White, Cathy Davis, Judith Harkins, Sue Von
Baeyer, Christina Essmana for supporting me

Fred Schloessinger, for holding me with love.

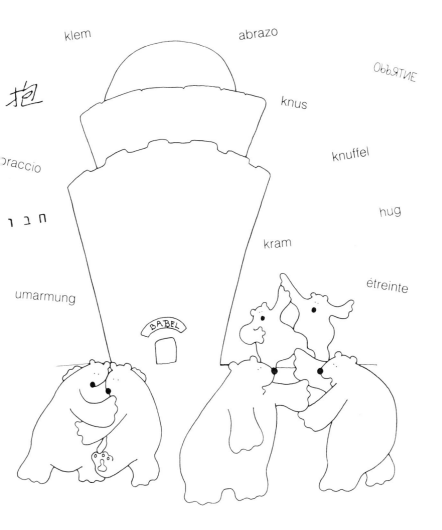

Hugs speak a universal language

communicate v.t.
1. To impart, pass along
2. To give or exchange information, thoughts, signals, or messages
3. To be connected

hug v.t.
1. To clasp or hold closely, especially in one's arms; embrace or enfold, as in affection
2. To cherish, hold fast
3. To keep very close

hug n.
An affectionate embrace (from Scandinavian, akin to old Norse *hugga,* to comfort, console)

hug therapy n.
1. The practice of administering hugs for the purpose of curing or healing, or of preserving health
2. Treatment of dis-ease through the simple, physical means of hugging

# About speaking with hugs

*Sorry*

*Thanks*

*Hello*

*Au Revoir*

*Peace*

*Whoopee*

# Theory

Science and instinct tell us that one good way to reach the sensitive living spirit is through physical touch. And one of the most important forms of touch is a hug. With a hug, we communicate as individuals on the deepest level. With a hug, we embrace the whole of life.

We all have an inner yearning that calls us to respond with a quality of contact that affirms our potential as growing individuals. The language of hugs nourishes the spirit.

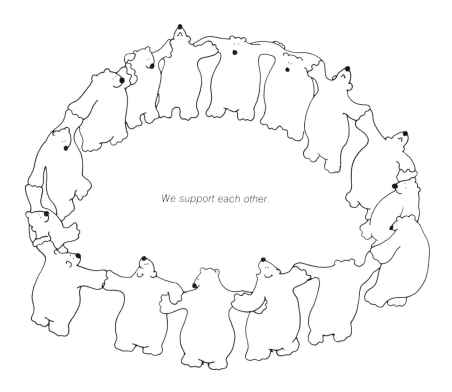

*We support each other.*

An embrace creates a circle of compassion that promotes
growth and healing and feeds our empty hearts.

# Rationale

Because we move about in a world of many languages, only the nonverbal language of touching and hugs knows no limits.

Because we live in an age of reason and technology, we are losing awareness of our senses. When we touch and hold each other in a spirit of compassion, we bring life to our senses and reaffirm our trust in our own feelings.

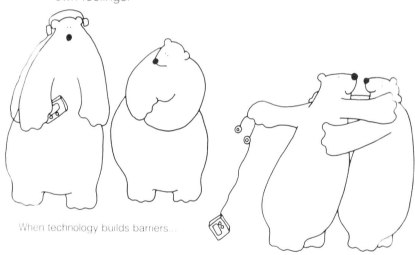

When technology builds barriers...

a hug tears them down

# **A**pplication

Say it with hugs to emphasize the message.

We may say aloud, "Let me know if there's any way I can help." A hug adds, *I really mean that!*

We may say aloud, "I like you." A hug adds, *I care deeply about you. In fact, I love you a lot.*

Punctuate with a hug!

Say it with hugs when words are awkward or hard to say.

We may know the appropriate words but find them really difficult to say out loud, especially if we're shy or overwhelmed by feelings. At such times we count on the language of hugs.

A hug can say things like:

*I am here for you any time.*

*I really understand your feelings.*

*Please celebrate my joy with me.*

*Allow me to share in your sadness.*

Even ordinary words like hello and goodbye are sometimes very hard to say.

Please let me help you bear this frightening time.

Say it with hugs when words can't express it.

Although we may speak from our most authentic selves as we reach into our deepest feelings, talk can only go so far. An embrace from the heart often cannot be translated into words.

When we allow ourselves to be in a still place of inner awareness, the message of vitality, spirit, and love that we all carry within us is often felt, given, and received in a place beyond language. To reduce this experience to words, either inwardly or out loud, may diminish a very profound message.

Besides using the magnificent gift of language, we must also respect intuitive, wordless wisdom and listen with our hearts. That is how we hear the greater meaning of the mystery we have named love.

Hugs have their own language.

# **Q**ualifications

Anyone can be a hug therapist. Since hug therapy is a helping technique that benefits both therapists and clients, the qualifications for being a hug therapist and being a client are the same: just being. Hugging for health is a mutually healing process for all participants.

But as a hug therapist, you take responsibility to communicate a genuine feeling of care and compassion.

Any qualified hug therapist can further develop skill and confidence by learning the special language of hugs.

# Ethics

A healing hug never gives a mixed message. Instead, a hug always speaks authentically about who we are and what we feel; we need first to be in touch with ourselves before we can reach out to touch someone else. We are uncomfortable and confused when words say one thing and an embrace says another.

I feel just wonderful. Everything is A-okay.

*I'm really very sad.*

A hug never says *I blame you* or *I want to cause harm.*

We are all complex individuals trying to find fulfillment. We do not have a choice about how we feel, but we can choose what we say or do in response to feelings.

We can discover ways to meet our needs without blaming or harming ourselves or others. As hug therapists, our responsibility is to create and heal, not to harm or blame. We can no longer afford to view the world in terms of "good guys" and "bad guys."

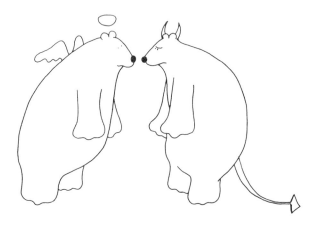

A therapeutic hug is always nonsexual.

A caring, supportive, or playful hug is different from a lover's embrace and does not invite the level of physical intimacy that is part of a romantic relationship.

*I want to be your lover, baby.*

*I want to be your friend.*

No.

Yes.

# **F**ee

Therapeutic touching is a new language that we are just learning. The price we pay in reaching out is that others may misinterpret our hugs as intrusive or conducive to a romantic relationship.

As we become more aware of what the language of touch can say to us about affirmation and support, we will discover that hugging is healthy communication that enriches our lives. As hugging becomes more acceptable as our "second language," the fees for risking will lessen accordingly.

*We are willing to risk a hug because the rewards are great.*

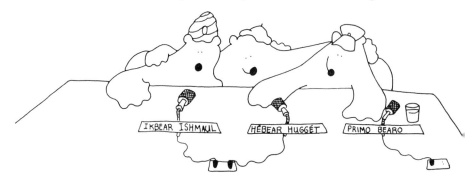

# Basics of hug language

Besides its particular message, a hug to be truly therapeutic always makes these nonverbal statements.

A therapeutic hug always says:

*I understand how you feel.*

Because we feel the same kinds of feelings, there is a bond of commonality that embraces us and creates unity. We respect our own feelings as a natural guidance system for making decisions, creating values, and working through problems. We validate each other's feelings as an essential part of being.

*Your loss is my loss.*

That's too bad.

A therapeutic hug always says:

*I respect your unique inner wisdom. You are special.*

We celebrate the fact that within the circle of unity are individuals whose rich diversity makes life exciting. Others' feelings, ideas, and values expand our reality beyond our limited and personal views. The world is full of endless possibilities because we are different.

A therapeutic hug always says:

*You are who you are, not just what you do.*

We all need the confirmation of ourselves as whole and unique beings separate from the many functional roles we must play.

Example: *You are not          only a doctor and a mother as well as a pitcher          in a softball league and a veterinary          assistant and an aerobics expert and an          arbiter of disputes and a lover          and a bus driver and a domestic          genius—you are YOU.*

*Have a hug. Clement.*

A review of the most often used hugs is helpful in order to choose just the right hug to convey the message. Each hug which follows has many verbal and nonverbal translations depending on the huggers and the situation; just a few are offered here.

# A dictionary of hugs

# **A**-frame hug

Classic. Somewhat formal. Beneficial to a wide range of huggers—from brides to board members, from graduating seniors to golden-age seniors.

An A-frame hug can say:

*I'd like to know you better.*

*Happy special occasion (whatever it may be)!*

*I know that you are dressed up for this festive event and would appreciate a hug that doesn't crush or wrinkle.*

# **A**nkle hug

Firm encirclement of another's ankle, usually by a hugger of small stature. Requires an immediate response, such as being picked up and given a bear hug. Differs from an ordinary tackle because of the hugger's feelings of love and need—and the huggee's feeling of warmth at being needed.

The ankle hug invariably says:

*I am smaller than you are now, and I count on you.*

*Just touching you gives me security.*

# Back-to-front hug

Or waist-grabber.

A joyful gesture of support, especially for those engaged in routine household or humdrum chores.

A waist-grabber imparts the message:

> *Don't be so intent on getting the job done that you forget how much we mean to each other.*
>
> *Friendship makes our workaday world go 'round.*

# **B**ear hug

Powerful. Secure. Use forbearance in making this hug
firm rather than breathless.

A sampling of bear hug messages:

*Let's both tap into the wonderful vitality we've been
given.*

*I support you 100 percent.*

*Life is an adventure—and you're a big part of its
newness and fun.*

# Cheek hug

Tender. Tasteful. Lightly given, it often has a spiritual quality.

A cheek hug can say:

*I recognize that you are feeling fragile.*

*I care about you.*

*May my genuine concern for you give you strength.*

# Custom-tailored hug

A creative, special-order hug. Takes into account setting, situation, principals, and what is needed from the hug. Sometimes, to please a particular hugger, a favorite pet or toy is included. A custom-tailored hug can say almost anything you like.

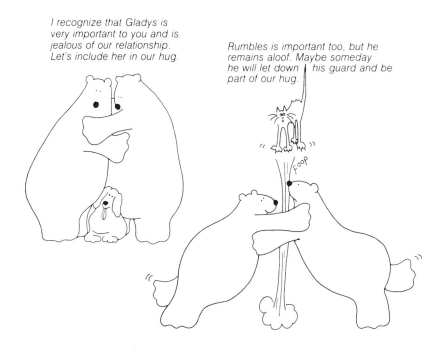

*I recognize that Gladys is very important to you and is jealous of our relationship. Let's include her in our hug.*

*Rumbles is important too, but he remains aloof. Maybe someday he will let down his guard and be part of our hug.*

# Grabber-squeezer hug

Playful, affectionate, brief. Offers the opportunity to work in a lot of fast hugging on a tight schedule. May be accompanied by a feeling of surprise.

A grabber-squeezer almost always says:

*HoHO! Let's never grow too old to play.*

*Even when responsibilities keep us hopping, fun is an essential part of our lives.*

*I'm in a terrible hurry, but this is a quick reminder that I really like you.*

# **G**roup hug

Popular for good friends or associates. Combines well with team sports or singing in parts.

A group hug tells everybody in it:

*We're all in this together.*

*One for all, and all for one.*

*Let's all share in the good feelings.*

# 'Guess who?' hug

A frolicsome hug for longtime friends. Makes a gentle game out of an ordinary "hello" or "good day" greeting.

A "guess who?" hug has this to say:

*If you guess who I am, I'll be happy you've thought about me. If you don't—well, mystery is part of the fun too.*

*We mustn't overlook the fact that humor is absolutely necessary for our well-being.*

# **H**eart-centered hug

Undistracted and unhurried. Perhaps the highest form of hugging. Acknowledges that place at the center of each of us where pure, unconditional love may be found.

A heart-centered hug says:

> *Feel our oneness as our bond of friendship grows.*
>
> *I may frown on your naughtiness or misbehavior, but I don't love you any less.*
>
> *Let's forgive each other—grudges are uncomfortable.*

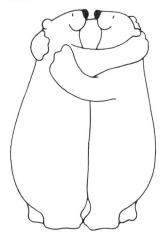

# **S**andwich hug

A three-way hug. Especially secure for the one in the middle.

Some messages of a sandwich hug:

*Let's affirm our deep feeling of family closeness.*

*We're all equal shareholders in this friendship.*

*Let's make sure none of us is ever left out.*

# Side-to-side hug

Also known as a lateral squeeze. A merry, playful aside. Use it while strolling together or waiting in line.

Listen to what a side-to-side hug has to say:

*Waiting around for gates to open is not a bit tedious because you're with me.*

*Being with you makes me feel good—wherever we are.*

# Top-of-the-head hug

Or cranial clasp.

Firm, supportive, strength-giving. Usually offered to a seated huggee by a standing hugger. A gift of power to one who is feeling stunned or frail or depressed.

The cranial clasp gives a clear message of strength:

*Tap into my positive energy if you are feeling helpless today.*

*I'm ready to share my strength with you for as long as you need it.*

# **V**ariations

Of course each basic hug type has numerous variations. If you are well-versed in these types and what each can say, you can augment your hug-message vocabulary limitlessly.

I'm here, Melissa.

Let's do hugs.

Scuba dooby doo.

You're really handy, Harriet.

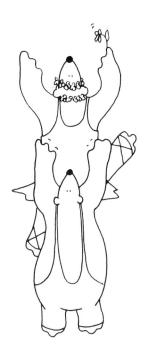

Pas de deux.

# Say it with hugs

As your hugging vocabulary grows, you will find that the wonderful language of hugs is perfectly adapted to conveying everyday messages, especially in the areas of communication which follow.

# Safety
# Security
# Trust

## A HUG SAYS SAFETY

Regardless of our age or status in life, we all need to feel safe. When we do not feel safe, our actions may become inefficient, our interactions with others may lose their pleasure.

A hug creates a warm circle of support so that we can return to our tasks with a renewed sense of safety.

A hug says, *In my arms is a place where you can feel safe.*

A hug-for-safety statement is needed:

when stepping up to a podium to give a talk
   a hug says, *No need for accordion knees—just imagine everyone in the audience giving you a safe hug.*

when graduating—from anywhere
   a hug says, *You will find safe places in your new life too.*

when the night is full of shifting shadows
   a hug says, *Daylight will show you that shadows are really the safe shapes of ordinary things.*

Try a heart-centered hug to shut out fears and pass along a message of safeness.

*You are safe here. Morning will come soon.*

A hug keeps back the shadows.

## A HUG SAYS SECURITY

Everyone needs to feel secure, but especially those on both ends of the age spectrum who depend on the love and good will of those who care for them.

A hug-for-security statement is needed:

by the very youngest trying out steps for the first time a hug says, *When the world you set out to explore seems frightening and complex, you can return any time to the security of my arms until you are ready to go out again and discover more.*

by the oldest trying out steps for the first time after
recovering from a fall

a hug says, *I will not allow you to become your
infirmity or lose your specialness or dignity or your
importance to me.*

Try a side-to-side or cheek hug to say security.

A HUG SAYS TRUST

Trust comes from the sense of security and safety we receive from others. Trust can free us to move when fear overwhelms our desire to participate in the exciting challenges of life.

Give a learn-to-trust hug message to:

a youth who needs reassurance that he is not alone in the difficult task of facing new responsibilities
  a hug says, *You do not have to do more or go faster or higher until you are ready. You can trust me to be here and support you through your journey into the adult world.*

a friend beginning a new venture in a new location with new associates
  a hug says, *Please take with you the feelings of trust you have learned here. I will continue to be your friend wherever you are.*

Sometimes a quick side-to-side hug is enough to reinforce a message of trust.

*If you start to tip over, I'll be here.*

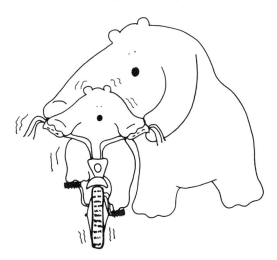

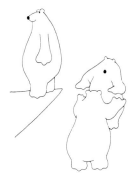

*You can trust us.*

*I trust you.*

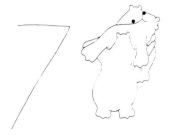

# **S**elf-worth

# **B**elonging

## A HUG SAYS SELF-WORTH

Self-worth is the foundation for satisfaction and success in our lives. This sense of personal value is created from the moment of birth, mostly by the messages others give us about ourselves.

Because the validation passed from generation to generation is often incomplete, many of us did not learn about our full worth when we were young. Now we have the chance to continue the process of affirmation, by giving the message through our hugs that we recognize the excellence of each individual.

A hug proclaims the innate worth of anyone:

a runner who does not quite qualify for a marathon,
an actress who muffs her lines,
a chef whose souffle flattens,
a batter who swings hard, but strikes out
  a hug says, *Self-worth and success are not synonyms. Trying is valuable. Being is valuable. Above all, YOU are valuable.*

one who has grown up with an uncomfortable sense of inadequacy, or even shame
  a hug says, *I have a real respect and affection for you. Please let me help you change your negative perceptions about yourself.*

Try a bear hug to pass along self-worth. (If the one you wish to hug is shy or fears intimacy, a gentler hug—like a cheek hug or a cranial clasp—may be more appropriate.)

*You are wonderful, worthy, noble, kind, and interesting.*

*Also huggable.*

## A HUG SAYS BELONGING

Our sense of worth expands when we feel we belong—
first to intimate groups of relatives and friends, then to
the amazing family of living creatures everywhere.

When we feel our place within the embrace of this
universal connection, our hugs invite others into the
circle of life.

When "I" becomes "we," a hug speaks ardently of the
warmth of belonging:

for anyone who is part of a group sharing an ideal, a
project, a common interest, a game, a trade or
profession—or who is lucky enough just to have a
bunch of good friends

*a hug says,Your separateness and my separateness
add something unique and wonderful to this team
we're part of.*

*This fellowship gives my life meaning.*

A group hug can be the greatest voice of all for
self-worth and belonging.

# Strength
# Healing

## A HUG SAYS STRENGTH

We often think of strength as a solitary energy that develops out of an individual's determination and toughness and self-responsibility. Of course responsibility-for-self is essential for personal power. But we can still pass along our inner vitality as a gift to others—to confirm and sustain their own strength and power.

Strength, particularly, is communicated as a bodily message. Touching and hugging are energizing. The wonder is: when we seek to transfer our energy in a hug, our own strength increases!

*Sometimes you lean on me.*

Give a gift-of-strength hug:

to someone left alone when a relationship dissolves
a hug says, *When your faith in others has been
damaged, let me hold you and fill you with strength.*

to a child feeling confused after a parent has moved
away from home
a hug says, *You are not responsible for your
parents' happiness. You have good friends in the
world outside—and I'm one of them.*

to a not-so-young athlete, retiring from the game
a hug says, *There are other strengths besides
physical prowess. I honor what you have achieved.
But most of all I really like who you are and who you
will be.*

A heart-centered or bear hug is a
strength-giving statement.

*Sometimes I lean on you.*

## A HUG SAYS HEALING

Our strength becomes a powerful healing force when
given through physical contact. We have heard
many-times-told stories of healing through touch. Now
scientific research continues to confirm that touching
and holding impart a life energy that heals—as well as
supports and comforts—those suffering from illness or
disease. New studies show that, to be truly therapeutic,
touching must be coupled with an intent to help and to
heal. Casual, offhand touching is less effective.

The vitality we receive from a therapeutic embrace
contains this healing message: *I am alive and whole
and I am coming home to my self.*

Give a healing hug to:

anyone who is trying to shake off an illness or infection or a bout with the blues, or whose broken body or spirit is mending

a hug says, *I will hold you so that you can draw strength from my support while you heal.*

*My strength combined with yours is more than the sum of both our strengths. Feel that remarkable energy flowing into making you whole again!*

A top-of-the-head hug speaks respectfully about healing.

*Though I have confidence in my own skill, I also respect the miracle of your self-healing. I recognize a healing force that is more powerful than either of us.*

Rx:

Four hugs a day for survival

Eight hugs a day for maintenance

Twelve hugs a day for growth

# Appreciation

# Happiness

# Celebration

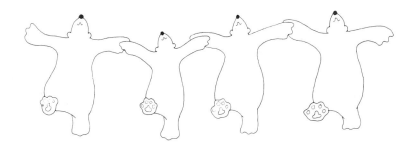

## A HUG SAYS APPRECIATION

Appreciation for others and gratitude for the abundance and variety of life—these are flavors of happiness we communicate in an embrace.

When we are filled with thankfulness and appreciation, our hugs proclaim, *I'm grateful today for the deliciousness of life. Let's be sure to take the time to taste the richness of each moment.*

Let a hug voice your appreciation for:

a favorite teacher
a hug says, *Thank you for making learning a never-ending adventure for me.*

a benefactor or a sponsor
a hug says, *I am grateful for the miracles you help bring about in my life.*

one who offers you a new contract or career
a hug says, *Thanks for the fresh challenge—and for your faith in me.*

a parent (now that you're grown up)
a hug says, *What a great experience to know you now as an adult friend!*

someone whose words have inspired you
    a hug says, *Your messages have brought me
    serenity and helped me grow spiritually.*

a comic or jester
    a hug says, *Thanks for your cleverness and creative
    clowning. You make us whole as you make us laugh.*

An appreciative hug can be any kind—from a
side-to-side to a waist-grabber—depending on the
degree of closeness you feel toward the huggee.

*I appreciate your humor.*

Hug a clown.

A HUG SAYS HAPPINESS

Wonder, excitement, humor, contentment, and serenity are some of the shades of happiness that color our lives. When we live under a rainbow of these good feelings, our hearts overflow with an abundance of joy—so much joy that we have trouble NOT sharing it!

It's a delight to communicate our pleasure with a hug that says, *What a great day! I'm feeling so alive and wonderful! I'm overjoyed to share the excitement of this moment with you!*

Pass on the exhilarating lyrics of a happiness hug to:

your cohort in the discovery of a new idea
    a hug says, *What's more exciting than exchanging thoughts and finding an entirely new concept that makes life's pieces fit together!*

your golf or tennis partner
a hug says, *It's really a kick—just to be here with you, moving freely and laughing over the crazy things that happen in a game.*

a new friend beside you in a beautiful place—a lakeside, a hilltop, a street at festival time
a hug says, Wow! *What a view! What a place! I'm excited that you can see it with me.*

A quick back-to-front hug or grabber-squeezer heralds your happiness.

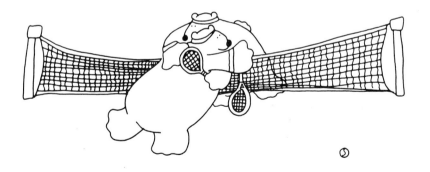

A HUG SAYS CELEBRATION

Celebration often means joining with others to share in the delight of a memorable event. We applaud and sing and feast and dance and laugh and cry at rituals that give meaning to our lives.

On these occasions we really need the language of hugs. A warm embrace is the happiest reward for a special moment, and says, *I am honored to be with you and to take part in these festivities.*

A back-to-front hug or bear hug, sandwich or group hug, custom-tailored or side-to-side hug—in fact, any kind of hug at all—sings out, *Let's celebrate!*

Yes!

But we don't have to wait for a special occasion to celebrate. We can celebrate who we are any time—here, now, sharing this world of marvels and miracles with those we care about.

We celebrate, too, our wonderful ability to communicate with hugs.

The language of hugs helps us speak from our hearts.

The language of hugs helps us see our true selves.

*You are not really a bear.*

*You are not a bear either.*

# That extra touch

All of us need not only hugs, but other kinds of respectful touching as well. For some, hugging may even be uncomfortable. It may cause feelings of distress or fear because of cultural conditioning, physical trauma, or emotional deprivation. Sometimes just gently holding a hand, or giving a validating pat on the back, a playful head rub, a relaxing neck massage, or a kind touch on the arm may be a more sensitive way to communicate support.

Remember, although touching and hugging are of extraordinary value, the most cherished gift we can give is our acceptance of others' unique feelings and needs. This means that our decision to communicate through hugs or touch must always be based on respect for what is comfortable for that person.

## About the author

Kathleen Keating, R.N., M.A., is a mental health counsellor and consultant in private practice. She conducts seminars and workshops on health and wellbeing, stress management, parent education, communication and problem-solving skills, and group dynamics. Her experience also includes biofeedback research and consulting and administration in therapeutic communities.

The theme of her life is, she says, "to feel, know, and teach the many dimensions of love: courage to struggle; vulnerability to give and to receive; sensitivity to compassion and the power of anger; openness to the delight of play and the deep, deep pleasure of a warm embrace".


## About the artist

Mimi Noland, designer of the gentle hug bears, is a 1982 graduate of Skidmore College with a major in psychology. She is a writer and singer, a horse breeder and trainer, and has completed training to become a licensed police officer. She is the author of a book, *I Never Saw the Sun Rise,* written at the age of fifteen under the pen name of Joan Donlan. She lives in Wayzata, Minnesota, on a farm with a houseful — and a barnful — of animals.